SUPPORTIVE PILLARS

in

Cultivating Children

Shaykh 'Abdur-Razzāq Ibn 'Abdul-Muḥsin al- 'Abbād al-Badr

ISBN: 978-1-6841-8854-3

First Edition: Muharram 1438 A.H. /October 2016 C.E.

Cover Design: Maktabatulirshad Publications

Translation by Abū Sulaymān Muḥammad ʿAbdul-ʿAẓīm Ibn Joshua Baker

Revision & Editing by ʿAbdullāh Omrān

Typesetting & formatting by Abū Sulaymān Muḥammad ʿAbdul-ʿAẓīm Ibn Joshua Baker

Printing: Ohio Printing

Subject: Family

Website: www.maktabatulirshad.com
E-mail: info@maktabatulirshad.com

Table of Contents

BRIEF BIOGRAPHY OF THE AUTHOR................4

TRANSLITERATION TABLE.....................7

INTRODUCTION........................10

SELECTING A RIGHTEOUS WIFE.............19

DUʿĀ (SUPPLICATION)...................21

CHOOSING GOOD NAMES................26

FAIRNESS.............................28

GENTLENESS AND COMPASSION..........31

SINCERE ADVICE AND GUIDANCE........34

THE RIGHTEOUS COMPANION...........41

AN EXCELLENT EXAMPLE................44

BRIEF BIOGRAPHY OF THE AUTHOR

His name: Shaykh ʿAbdur-Razzāq Ibn ʿAbdul-Muḥsin al-ʿAbbād al-Badr.

He is the son of the *ʿAllāmah* and *Muhaddith* of Madīnah Shaykh ʿAbdul-Muḥsin al ʿAbbād al-Badr.

Birth: He was born on the 22nd day of *Dhul-Qaʿdah* in the year 1382 AH in az-Zalʿfi, Kingdom of Saudi Arabia. He currently resides in Madīnah.

Current Occupation: He is a member of the teaching staff at the Islāmic University of Madīnah.

Scholarly Certifications: Doctorate in *ʿAqīdah*.

The Shaykh has authored books, papers of research, as well as numerous explanations in different disciplines. Among them are:

1. *Fiqh of Supplications & adh-Kār*.

2. *Hajj & Refinement of Souls*.

3. Explanation of 'Exemplary Principles' by Shaykh Ibn 'Uthaymīn (رحمهاللّٰه).

4. Explanation of the book, *The Principles of Names & Attributes*, authored by Shaykh-ul-Islām Ibn al-Qayyim (رحمهاللّٰه).

5. Explanation of the book, *Good Words*, authored by Shaykh-ul-Islām Ibn al-Qayyim (رحمهاللّٰه).

6. Explanation of the book, al-'Aqīdah *at-Tahāwiyyah*.

7. Explanation of the book, *Fusūl: Biography of the Messenger*, by Ibn Kathīr (رحمهاللّٰه).

8. An explanation of the book, *al-Adab-ul-Mufrad*, authored by Imām Bukhārī (رحمهاللّٰه).

He studied knowledge under a number of scholars. The most distinguished of them are:

1. His father the *'Allāmah* Shaykh 'Abdul-Muḥsin al-Badr (حفظه اللّٰه).

2. The *'Allāmah* Shaykh Ibn Bāz (رحمهاللّٰه).

3. The *'Allāmah* Shaykh Muḥammad Ibn Sāliḥ al-'Uthaymīn (رحمهاللّٰه).

4. Shaykh 'Alī Ibn Nāsir al-Faqīhi (حفظه الله).

TRANSLITERATION TABLE

<u>Consonants</u>

ء	'	د	d	ض	ḍ	ك	k
ب	b	ذ	dh	ط	ṭ	ل	l
ت	t	ر	r	ظ	ẓ	م	m
ث	th	ز	z	ع	'	ن	n
ج	j	س	s	غ	gh	هـ	h
ح	ḥ	ش	sh	ف	f	و	w
خ	kh	ص	ṣ	ق	q	ي	y

<u>Vowels</u>

Short	́-	a	-̣	i	́-	u
Long	اـ	ā	ـي	ī	ـُو	ū

Diphthongs	ـَو	aw	ـَي	ay

Arabic Symbols & their meanings

حفظه الله	May Allāh preserve him
رَضِوَٱللَّهُعَنْهُ	May Allāh be pleased with him (i.e. a male companion of the Prophet Muḥammad)
سُبْحَانَهُوَتَعَالَى	Glorified & Exalted is Allāh
عَزَّوَجَلَّ	(Allāh) the Mighty & Sublime
تَبَارَكَوَتَعَالَى	(Allāh) the Blessed & Exalted
جَلَّوَعَلَا	(Allāh) the Sublime & Exalted
عَلَيْهِٱلصَّلَاةُوَٱلسَّلَامُ	May Allāh send Blessings & Safety upon him (i.e. a Prophet or Messenger)
صَلَّىٱللَّهُعَلَيْهِوَعَلَىٰآلِهِوَسَلَّمَ	May Allāh send Blessings & Safety upon him and his family (i.e. Du'ā sent when mentioning the Prophet Muḥammad)

رَحِمَهُ ٱللَّهُ	May Allāh have mercy upon him
رَضِيَاللَّهُعَنْهُمْ	May Allāh be pleased with them (i.e. Du'ā made for the Companions of the Prophet Muḥammad)
جَلَّجَلَالُهُ	(Allāh) His Majesty is Exalted
رَضِيَاللَّهُعَنْهَا	May Allāh be pleased with her (i.e. a female companion of the Prophet Muḥammad)

INTRODUCTION

All praise belongs to Allāh, the Lord of all that exists. May Allāh raise the rank of His servant and grant His Messenger, and close friend—our Prophet Muḥammad—and his family and all of his Companions peace.

To proceed:

Verily, among the utmost important obligations and enormous trusts that the servant has been obliged to have great concern for in this life is his children, particularly regarding cultivating, disciplining, advising and giving them directives.

Indeed, children are the total sum of an enormous trust that Allāh (عَزَّوَجَلَّ) commands (us) to observe and preserve when He (سُبْحَانَهُوَتَعَالَى) mentions the qualities of the believers,

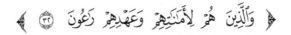

"**And those who keep their trusts and covenants;**" [*Sūrah al-Ma'arij* 70:32]

He (سُبْحَانَهُوَتَعَالَى) also states,

﴿ يَـٰٓأَيُّهَا ٱلَّذِينَ ءَامَنُواْ لَا تَخُونُواْ ٱللَّهَ وَٱلرَّسُولَ وَتَخُونُواْ أَمَـٰنَـٰتِكُمۡ وَأَنتُمۡ تَعۡلَمُونَ ﴿٢٧﴾ ﴾

"O you who believe! Betray not Allāh and His Messenger, nor betray knowingly your *Amānāt* (things entrusted to you, and all the duties which Allāh has ordained for you)." [*Sūrah al-Anfāl* 8:27]

Just as Allāh (سُبْحَانَهُوَتَعَالَى) bestows upon parents this tremendous blessing, He says,

﴿ لِّلَّهِ مُلۡكُ ٱلسَّمَـٰوَٰتِ وَٱلۡأَرۡضِۚ يَخۡلُقُ مَا يَشَآءُۚ يَهَبُ لِمَن يَشَآءُ إِنَـٰثًا وَيَهَبُ لِمَن يَشَآءُ ٱلذُّكُورَ ﴿٤٩﴾ ﴾

"To Allāh belongs the kingdom of the heavens and the earth. He creates what He wills. He bestows female (offspring) upon whom He wills and bestows male (offspring) upon whom He wills." [*Sūrah ash-Shura* 42:49]

He has conferred this blessing upon them, and He has made incumbent upon them certain rights and obligations; He has also made it as a test for the parents.

If they establish those rights concerning their children as Allāh (سُبْحَانَهُوَتَعَالَى) ordered them to do, then they will have a great reward and a plentiful recompense with Allāh. However, if they neglect it, then they have subjected themselves to punishment according to their level of neglect.

Allāh (سُبْحَانَهُوَتَعَالَى) says,

﴿ يَٰٓأَيُّهَا ٱلَّذِينَ ءَامَنُواْ قُوٓاْ أَنفُسَكُمۡ وَأَهۡلِيكُمۡ نَارًا وَقُودُهَا ٱلنَّاسُ وَٱلۡحِجَارَةُ عَلَيۡهَا مَلَٰٓئِكَةٌ غِلَاظٌ شِدَادٌ ﴾

"O you who believe! Ward off from yourselves and your families a Fire (Hell) whose fuel is men and stones, over which are (appointed) angels stern (and) severe." [*Sūrah at-Tahreem* 66:6]

This verse is a great foundation concerning the obligation of guardianship, cultivation, and the giving of serious attention towards the children.

'Ali ibn Abī Talib (رَضِيَاللَّهُعَنْهُ) said explaining this verse:

عَـلِّـمُـوهُـمْ، وَ أَدِّبُـوهُـمْ

"Teach and discipline them."[1]

An emphasis of this command and a clarification of its duty upon the parents has been authentically reported from the Prophet (صَلَّىاللَّهُعَلَيْهِوَسَلَّمَ) when he said,

كُلُّكُمْ رَاعٍ وَكُلُّكُمْ مَسْئُولٌ، فَالإِمَامُ رَاعٍ وَهُوَ مَسْئُولٌ وَالرَّجُلُ رَاعٍ عَلَى أَهْلِهِ وَهُوَ مَسْئُولٌ وَالْمَرْأَةُ رَاعِيَةٌ عَلَى بَيْتِ زَوْجِهَا وَهْىَ مَسْئُولَةٌ، وَالْعَبْدُ رَاعٍ عَلَى مَالِ سَيِّدِهِ وَهُوَ مَسْئُولٌ، أَلاَ فَكُلُّكُمْ رَاعٍ وَكُلُّكُمْ مَسْئُولٌ عَنْ رَعِيَّتِهِ .

---

[1] In the book authored by at-Tabari *Jāmi' al-Bayān fi ta'wīl al-Qur'ān* (23/103).

"Every one of you is a guardian, and every one of you is responsible (for his wards). A ruler is a guardian and is responsible (for his subjects); a man is a guardian of his family and responsible (for them); a wife is a guardian of her husband's house, and she is responsible (for it); a slave is a guardian of his master's property and is responsible (for that). Beware! All of you are guardians and are responsible (for your wards)." [2]

The Prophet's (ﷺ) statement, **"responsible"** is a reminder that Allāh (جَلَّجَلَالُه) will question the servant concerning these trusts when the servant stands in front of Allāh on the Day of Resurrection. Some of the people of knowledge have also said,

"Indeed Allāh (سُبْحَانَهُوَتَعَالَى) will question the father about his son on the Day of Resurrection before He asks the son about his father. Surely just as the father has rights over his son, the son has rights over his father." [3]

---

[2] Collected by al-Bukhārī (5188); and Muslim (1829).
[3] In the book authored by Ibn al-Qayyim (رَحِمَهُاللَّه) *Tuhfatul-Mawdūd bi Ahkaam al-Mawlūd* (page 229).

Ibn ʿUmar (رَضِيَاللَّهُعَنْهُمَا) also stated about the Ḥadīth,

أَدِّبْ ابْنَكَ فَإِنَّكَ مَسْؤُولٌ عَنْ وَلَدِكَ ؛ مَـاذَا
أَدَّبْتَهُ، وَ مَـاذَا عَلَّمْتَهُ، وَ إِنَّهُ مَسْؤُولٌ عَـنْ
بِـرِّكَ وَ طَـوَاعِـيَـتِـهِ لَـكَ .

"Discipline your son, for indeed you are responsible for him. You will be asked, 'What did you instruct him to do? What did you teach him? Indeed, he will be asked about his good kindness and obedience towards you."[4]

Just as Allāh (سُبْحَانَهُوَتَعَالَى) has ordered children to be dutiful to their parents and has made it an obligation to treat them with kindness with His statement,

﴿ وَوَصَّيْنَا ٱلْإِنسَٰنَ بِوَٰلِدَيْهِ حُسْنًا ﴾

"And We have enjoined on man to be good and dutiful to his parents." [*Sūrah al-Ankabut 29:8*]

---

[4] In the book authored by al-Bayhaqī *as-Sunan al-Kubrā* (#5301).

Indeed, Allāh has ordered the parents concerning cultivating them and educating them as He (سُبْحَانَهُوَتَعَالَى) says,

$$﴿ يُوصِيكُمُ ٱللَّهُ فِى أَوْلَـٰدِكُمْ ﴾$$

"Allāh commands you as regards your children's (inheritance)." [*Sūrah an-Nisā'* 4:11]

Our Noble Prophet (صَلَّىٰاللَّهُعَلَيْهِوَسَلَّمَ) informed us that the parents have an enormous influence over their children; in their beliefs and way of life, and especially in their morals and natural disposition. He (صَلَّىٰاللَّهُعَلَيْهِوَسَلَّمَ) said,

$$كُلُّ مَوْلُودٍ يُولَدُ عَلَى الْفِطْرَةِ، فَأَبَوَاهُ يُهَوِّدَانِهِ أَوْ يُنَصِّرَانِهِ أَوْ$$

$$يُمَجِّسَانِهِ، كَمَثَلِ الْبَهِيمَةِ تُنْتَجُ الْبَهِيمَةَ، هَلْ تَرَى فِيهَا$$

$$جَدْعَاءَ$$

"Every child is born with a true faith of Islām (i.e. to worship none but Allāh Alone) and his parents convert him to Judaism or Christianity or Magianism, as an animal

delivers a perfect baby animal. Do you find it mutilated?"[5]

This is a profound and tangible example. Indeed, an animal normally delivers healthy animals free of defect and disease. It doesn't have any mutilation or a severed hand, ear or foot. That only happens on the part of the animal's owner or guardian, either due to neglect or by action taken directly against the animal.

Likewise, the child is born with the true faith of Islām. When he is taught lying, deception, corruption, depravity or any other evil act, then this goes outside the natural disposition (i.e., Fitrah). This is either caused by poor upbringing, neglect or outside influences from wicked people or companions.

Based upon the importance of this trust and its magnitude, I will mention the utmost significant supporting pillars and foundations which are necessary for every parent to give great concern to in

---

[5] Collected by al-Bukhārī (5188); and Muslim (1829).

order to actualize this magnanimous demand and lofty goal.

SELECTING A RIGHTEOUS WIFE

Surely, the first of the supportive pillars in cultivating children is selecting a righteous wife and this takes place before children are born. You are obliged to be diligent in selecting a wife known for her righteousness, integrity and piety because she will be your aid in cultivating, educating, and upbringing the children upon righteousness. Even if the righteous wife doesn't aid in cultivating the children, she will never be a harm to them in their religion or moral character.

Based upon this, an encouragement comes from our Noble Prophet (ﷺ) to select the righteous woman. He (ﷺ) said,

تُنْكَحُ الْمَرْأَةُ لِأَرْبَعِ لِمَالِهَا وَلِحَسَبِهَا وَلِجَمَالِهَا وَلِدِينِهَا فَاظْفَرْ بِذَاتِ الدِّينِ تَرِبَتْ يَدَاكَ

"A woman may be married for four reasons: for her property, her status. her beauty and

her religion, so try to get one who is religious, may your hand be smeared with dust." [6]

---

[6] Collected by al-Bukhārī (#5090); and Muslim (#1466)

DUʿĀ (SUPPLICATION)

From the utmost important of these supportive pillars is supplicating for one's children. This supplication begins before their existence and continues after they are born. The parents should supplicate that Allāh (سُبْحَانَهُوَتَعَالَى) blesses them with righteous offspring. After they are born, they should also supplicate for the children that Allāh guides them and makes them righteous and firm upon the religion. This is an example taken from the Prophets (عَلَيْهِمُالسَّلَامُ), just as Allāh (سُبْحَانَهُوَتَعَالَى) informs us about His close friend, ʾIbrāhīm (عَلَيْهِالسَّلَامُ) that he said,

$$ ﴿ \; رَبِّ هَبْ لِي مِنَ ٱلصَّٰلِحِينَ \; ۝ \; ﴾ $$

"My Lord! Grant me (offspring) from the righteous." [Sūrah as-Ṣāffāt 37:100]

ʾIbrāhīm also said,

$$ ﴿ \; رَبِّ ٱجْعَلْنِي مُقِيمَ ٱلصَّلَوٰةِ وَمِن ذُرِّيَّتِي \; ﴾ $$

"O, my Lord! Make me one who performs *As-Ṣalāh* (*Iqamat-as-Ṣalāh*), and (also) from my offspring." [*Sūrah 'Ibrāhīm* 14:40]

In the same fashion, it was said about Zakarīyā (عَلَيْهِ ٱلسَّلَامُ),

﴿ هُنَالِكَ دَعَا زَكَرِيَّا رَبَّهُۥ قَالَ رَبِّ هَبۡ لِى مِن لَّدُنكَ ذُرِّيَّةً طَيِّبَةً إِنَّكَ سَمِيعُ ٱلدُّعَآءِ ۝ ﴾

"At that time Zakarīyā invoked his Lord, saying: "O my Lord! Grant me from You, a good offspring. You are indeed the All-Hearer of invocation." [*Sūrah Āli 'Imrān* 3:38]

Among the supplications of the servants of Ar-Raḥmān (i.e., the Most Gracious) whom the Lord of all that exists praises, they say,

﴿ وَٱلَّذِينَ يَقُولُونَ رَبَّنَا هَبۡ لَنَا مِنۡ أَزۡوَٰجِنَا وَذُرِّيَّٰتِنَا قُرَّةَ أَعۡيُنٍ وَٱجۡعَلۡنَا لِلۡمُتَّقِينَ إِمَامًا ۝ ﴾

"Our Lord! Bestow on us from our wives and our offspring who will be the comfort of our

eyes, and make us leaders for the *Muttaqūn.*"
[*Sūrah al-Furqān* 25:74]

Among Allāh's blessings and bounties is that He
(عَزَّوَجَلَّ) causes the father's supplication for his
children to be answered and not rejected, just as it
was affirmed by the Messenger of Allāh (صَلَّى ٱللَّهُ عَلَيْهِ وَسَلَّمَ)
when he said,

ثَلَاثُ دَعَوَاتٍ مُسْتَجَابَاتٌ لاَ شَكَّ فِيهِنَّ دَعْوَةُ الْوَالِدِ
وَدَعْوَةُ الْمُسَافِرِ وَدَعْوَةُ الْمَظْلُومِ

**"Three supplications are answered, there
being no doubt about them; that of a father,
that of a traveler and that of one who has been
wronged."** 7

In this instance, it is imperative that we pay close
attention to the importance of both parents being
very cautious from supplicating against their
children, especially in moments of anger. They

---

7 Collected by Abū Dāwud in his book *as-Sunan;* and at-Tirmidhī
in his book *al-Jāmi'* (#1905) from the Ḥadīth of Abū Hurayrah
(رَضِيَ ٱللَّهُ عَنْهُ); and Shaykh al-Albānī authenticated it in his book *as-
Ṣaḥīḥah* (#597).

should not be hasty in supplicating against them lest it is answered and, afterwards, they are full of remorse.

Our Noble Messenger (ﷺ) warned us from that when he said,

لاَ تَدْعُوا عَلَى أَنْفُسِكُمْ وَلاَ تَدْعُوا عَلَى أَوْلاَدِكُمْ وَلاَ تَدْعُوا عَلَى أَمْوَالِكُمْ لاَ تُوَافِقُوا مِنَ اللهِ سَاعَةً يُسْأَلُ فِيهَا عَطَاءٌ فَيَسْتَجِيبُ لَكُمْ

"Do not invoke curses on yourself or on your children or on your possessions lest you should happen to do it at a moment when the supplications are accepted, and your prayer might be granted." [8]

Allāh (سُبْحَانَهُوَتَعَالَى) says,

﴿ وَيَدْعُ ٱلْإِنسَٰنُ بِٱلشَّرِّ دُعَآءَهُۥ بِٱلْخَيْرِ وَكَانَ ٱلْإِنسَٰنُ عَجُولًا ١١ ﴾

---

[8] Collected by Muslim in his Ṣaḥīḥ (#3009).

"And man invokes (Allāh) for evil as he invokes (Allāh) for good and man is ever hasty." [*Sūrah al-Isrā'* 17:11]

Qatādah (رَحِمَهُ ٱللَّهُ) said about this verse,

يَـدْعُو عَلَى مَالِهِ؛ فَيَلْعَنُ مَالَهُ وَ وَلَدَهُ، وَ لَوْ اسْتَجَابَ

اللهُ لَهُ لَأَهْلَكَهُ.

"Man invokes curses on his wealth; so he curses wealth and children. Even if Allāh answers his supplication, he will be ruined."
9

Al-Allamah 'Abdur Raḥmān as-Sa'dī (رَحِمَهُ ٱللَّهُ), commenting on this verse, said,

"This is from the ignorance and hastiness of man where he invokes curses on himself, his children, and his wealth when angry; so he hastens to invoke curses just as he invokes for good."10

---

9 In the book authored by at-Ṭabarī, *Jāmi' al-Bayān fi ta'wīl al-Qur'ān* (14/513).
10 In the book *Taysīr al-Karīm al-Mannān* (page 454).

CHOOSING GOOD NAMES

Among the matters which aid in cultivating children upon righteousness is that both parents choose good, wholesome names for their children which will attach them to the obedience of Allāh (سُبْحَانَهُ وَتَعَالَى) like naming him, **"'Abdullāh, 'Abdur Raḥmān, Muḥammad, or Ṣālih"** and similar to these beautiful names that remind him of his connection to righteousness, worship, and what is praiseworthy.

In most cases, that will have an influence on him as it is stated, **"Every man has a share from his name."**

This was affirmed from the Prophet (صَلَّى ٱللَّهُ عَلَيْهِ وَسَلَّمَ) when he said,

إِنَّ أَحَبَّ أَسْمَائِكُمْ إِلَى اللَّهِ عَبْدُ اللَّهِ وَعَبْدُ الرَّحْمَنِ

"The names most beloved to Allāh are 'Abdullāh and 'Abdur ar-Raḥmān." [11]

---

[11] Collected by Muslim in his Ṣaḥīḥ (#2132).

From what is appropriate is that the father explains to his son the meaning of his name and the reason for this name being beloved to Allāh (جَلَّجَلَالُهُ). For example, if his name is ʿAbdullāh (i.e., the servant of Allāh), then he should say to him, **"You are a servant of Allāh whom He has created, brought you into existence and has bestowed on you many bounties which necessitate from you that you show gratitude and obedience to Him (i.e., Allāh)"** and similar to this type of speech.

FAIRNESS

Indeed, among these great supportive pillars in cultivating children is having fairness among them and being far removed from discrimination, inequity and injustice. Whenever the father is not fair amongst his children, it brings about enmity, mutual jealousy and hatred. On the other hand, if he persists in being fair to them all, then that is among the greatest means for them mutually having love and friendship for each other as well as dutifulness to him (i.e., the father).

It is mentioned in Ṣaḥīḥ al-Bukhārī on the authority of N'umān bin Bashīr (رَضِيَاللَّهُعَنْهُ) that his father gave him a gift and his mother requested that his father call the Messenger of Allāh (صَلَّىاللَّهُعَلَيْهِوَسَلَّمَ) as a witness for that. So when the Messenger of Allāh (صَلَّىاللَّهُعَلَيْهِوَسَلَّمَ) arrived, he said to him (i.e., the father),

أَعْطَيْتَ سَائِرَ وَلَدِكَ مِثْلَ هَذَا ". قَالَ لاَ. قَالَ صَلَّى اللهُ عَلَيْهِ وَ سَلَّم: " فَاتَّقُوا اللَّهَ، وَاعْدِلُوا بَيْنَ أَوْلاَدِكُمْ

"Have you given (the like of it) to every one of your sons?' He replied in the negative. Allāh's Messenger (ﷺ) said, 'Have Taqwā of Allāh, and be just to your children.'"[12]

In another wording of the Ḥadīth,

لاَ أَشْهَدُ عَلَى جَوْرٍ

"I will not bear witness to unfairness."[13]

In another wording from Imām Muslim, it is said that the Prophet (ﷺ) said to him,

أَيَسُرُّكَ أَنْ يَكُونُوا إِلَيْكَ فِي الْبِرِّ سَوَاءً " . قَالَ بَلَى . قَالَ "

فَلاَ إِذًا.

"Do you not expect goodness from all of them as you expect from him?" He said, "Yes, of course." The Messenger of Allāh (ﷺ)

---

[12] Collected by al-Bukhārī in his Ṣaḥīḥ (#2587).
[13] Collected by al-Bukhārī in his Ṣaḥīḥ (#2650); and Muslim in his Ṣaḥīḥ (#1623).

said, "Then don't do this (i.e., do not give a gift to one son only)."[14]

This is a clear warning from inequity and injustice amongst the children and it is a clarification of what causes disrespect (i.e., to the parents), the lack of dutifulness, severance of mutual relations and abandonment among children.

---

[14] Collected by Muslim in his Ṣaḥīḥ (#1623).

GENTLENESS AND COMPASSION

Among the supportive pillars in cultivating children is gentleness and kindness towards them as well as treating them with compassion and beneficence while being cautious and distant from harshness, vehemence, and roughness, as the Prophet (صَلَّى ٱللَّهُ عَلَيْهِ وَسَلَّمَ) said,

إِنَّ الرِّفْقَ لاَ يَكُونُ فِي شَىْءٍ إِلاَّ زَانَهُ وَلاَ يُنْزَعُ مِنْ شَىْءٍ إِلاَّ شَانَهُ

"Gentleness is not to be found in anything but that it adds to its beauty and it is not withdrawn from anything, but it makes it defective." [15]

This compassion and gentleness must be initiated from the time of their earliest youth and progress and continue. Surely, this is a means for the children to be close to their father and have a love for him. With this closeness and love it becomes easy to direct

---

[15] Collected by Muslim in his Ṣaḥīḥ (#2594).

the children towards good and advise them. In this fashion, they will comply and accept the advice.

The texts from the Prophet's Sunnah (ﷺ) clarifying this supportive pillar are increasingly abundant and it is mentioned on the authority of Abū Hurayrah (رضي الله عنه) that the Prophet (ﷺ) kissed Ḥasan bin 'Ali (رضي الله عنه) while al-Aqr'a bin Ḥābis (رضي الله عنه) was sitting with him and he said,

إِنَّ لِي عَشَرَةً مِنَ الْوَلَدِ مَا قَبَّلْتُ وَاحِدًا مِنْهُمْ فَقَالَ رَسُولُ اللَّهِ صَلَّى اللهُ عَلَيْهِ وَ سَلَّمَ : " إِنَّهُ مَنْ لاَ يَرْحَمْ لاَ يُرْحَمْ

"I have ten children, but I have never kissed any one of them, whereupon Allāh's Messenger (ﷺ) said: 'He who does not show mercy, no mercy would be shown to him.'" [16]

On the authority of the Mother of the believers, 'Āishah (رضي الله عنها) said,

---

[16] Collected by al-Bukhārī in his Ṣaḥīḥ (#5997); and Muslim collected it in His Ṣaḥīḥ (#2594).

جَاءَ أَعْرَابِيٌّ إِلَى النَّبِيِّ صَلَّى اللهُ عَلَيْهِ وَ سَلَّمَ فَقَالَ تُقَبِّلُونَ

الصِّبْيَانَ فَمَا نُقَبِّلُهُمْ. فَقَالَ النَّبِيُّ صَلَّى اللهُ عَلَيْهِ وَ سَلَّمَ

: أَوَ أَمْلِكُ لَكَ أَنْ نَزَعَ اللَّهُ مِنْ قَلْبِكَ الرَّحْمَةَ

"A Bedouin came to the Prophet (ﷺ) and said to him, 'Messenger of Allāh, do you kiss children? By Allāh, we do not kiss them.' The Messenger of Allāh (ﷺ) said, 'Can I put mercy in your heart after Allāh has removed it?'" [17]

---

[17] Collected by al-Bukhārī in his Ṣaḥīḥ (#5998).

SINCERE ADVICE AND GUIDANCE

Also among the tremendous supportive pillars in cultivating children is perseverance in giving sincere advice and guidance, especially towards the lofty matters and noble characteristics. Start by teaching them the Islāmic beliefs, religious obligations, and its pillars, as well as the rest of legislative commands. In the same manner, when dealing with reprimands and warnings, start with the major sins and crimes, and then the rest of the legislative prohibitions.

These matters necessitate a major portion of giving guidance and sincere advice. Afterwards, the father and mother should direct their focus onto matters which will make good the situation for their children in this worldly life from food and clothing, etc.

Among the profound and beneficial advices which direct to the correct way of advising is what Allāh (عَزَّوَجَلَّ) mentions in His book concerning Luqmān, the Wise. When he admonished his son in Sūrah Luqmān, he began with Tawhīd and then mentioned twice the command to be dutiful to both parents.

After that, he pointed out Allāh's encompassment (عَزَّوَجَلَّ) of His creation.

Within his advice is an indication of the dire need of understanding that Allāh (جَلَّجَلَالُهُ) is consistently observing all of his actions. Furthermore, Luqmān urges his son to establish the Ṣalāh which is the greatest physical deed (one performs) and he concluded his advice with pointing out to his son, in summary, sublime morals and lofty matters.

Allāh (سُبْحَانَهُوَتَعَالَى) says,

﴿ وَإِذْ قَالَ لُقْمَٰنُ لِٱبْنِهِۦ وَهُوَ يَعِظُهُۥ يَٰبُنَىَّ لَا تُشْرِكْ بِٱللَّهِ إِنَّ ٱلشِّرْكَ لَظُلْمٌ عَظِيمٌ ۝ وَوَصَّيْنَا ٱلْإِنسَٰنَ بِوَٰلِدَيْهِ حَمَلَتْهُ أُمُّهُۥ وَهْنًا عَلَىٰ وَهْنٍ وَفِصَٰلُهُۥ فِى عَامَيْنِ أَنِ ٱشْكُرْ لِى وَلِوَٰلِدَيْكَ إِلَىَّ ٱلْمَصِيرُ ۝ وَإِن جَٰهَدَاكَ عَلَىٰٓ أَن تُشْرِكَ بِى مَا لَيْسَ لَكَ بِهِۦ عِلْمٌ فَلَا تُطِعْهُمَا وَصَاحِبْهُمَا فِى ٱلدُّنْيَا مَعْرُوفًا وَٱتَّبِعْ سَبِيلَ مَنْ أَنَابَ إِلَىَّ ثُمَّ إِلَىَّ مَرْجِعُكُمْ فَأُنَبِّئُكُم بِمَا

كُنتُمۡ تَعۡمَلُونَ ۝ يَٰبُنَىَّ إِنَّهَآ إِن تَكُ مِثۡقَالَ حَبَّةٖ مِّنۡ خَرۡدَلٖ فَتَكُن فِى صَخۡرَةٍ أَوۡ فِى ٱلسَّمَٰوَٰتِ أَوۡ فِى ٱلۡأَرۡضِ يَأۡتِ بِهَا ٱللَّهُۚ إِنَّ ٱللَّهَ لَطِيفٌ خَبِيرٞ ۝ يَٰبُنَىَّ أَقِمِ ٱلصَّلَوٰةَ وَأۡمُرۡ بِٱلۡمَعۡرُوفِ وَٱنۡهَ عَنِ ٱلۡمُنكَرِ وَٱصۡبِرۡ عَلَىٰ مَآ أَصَابَكَۖ إِنَّ ذَٰلِكَ مِنۡ عَزۡمِ ٱلۡأُمُورِ ۝ وَلَا تُصَعِّرۡ خَدَّكَ لِلنَّاسِ وَلَا تَمۡشِ فِى ٱلۡأَرۡضِ مَرَحًاۖ إِنَّ ٱللَّهَ لَا يُحِبُّ كُلَّ مُخۡتَالٖ فَخُورٖ ۝ وَٱقۡصِدۡ فِى مَشۡيِكَ وَٱغۡضُضۡ مِن صَوۡتِكَۚ إِنَّ أَنكَرَ ٱلۡأَصۡوَٰتِ لَصَوۡتُ ٱلۡحَمِيرِ ۝

"And (remember) when Luqmān said to his son when he was advising him: "O my son! Join not in worship others with Allāh. Verily! Joining others in worship with Allāh is a great *Zulm* (wrong) indeed. And We have enjoined on man (to be dutiful and good) to his parents. His mother bore him in weakness and hardship upon weakness and hardship, and his weaning is in two years. Give thanks to Me and to your parents, unto Me is the final destination. But if they (both) strive with you to make you join in worship with Me others that of which you have no knowledge, then obey them not, but behave with them in the world kindly, and follow the path of him who turns to Me in repentance and in obedience. Then to Me will be your return, and I shall tell you what you used to do. O, my son! If it is (anything) equal to the weight of a grain of mustard-seed, and though it is on a rock, or in the heavens or in the earth, Allāh will bring it forth. Verily, Allāh is Subtle (in bringing out that grain), Well-Aware (of its place). O, my son! *Aqim-is-Ṣalāh* (perform *As-Ṣalāh*), enjoin (people) for *Al-Ma'ruf* (Islāmic Monotheism and all that is good), and forbid (people) from *Al-Munkar* (i.e. disbelief in the Oneness of Allāh, polytheism of all kinds and all that is evil and bad), and bear with patience whatever befall you. Verily! These are some of the important commandments ordered by Allāh with no exemption. And turn not your face away from men with pride,

nor walk in insolence through the earth.
Verily, Allāh likes not each arrogant boaster.
And be moderate (or show no insolence) in
your walking, and lower your voice. Verily,
the harshest of all voices is the voice (braying)
of the ass." [*Sūrah Luqmān* 31:13-19]

The Prophets and the righteous followed this course
of action as it was mentioned in the previous advice
of Luqmān. Allāh (جَلَّجَلَالُهُ) mentions about His
Prophets, 'Ibrāhīm and Yaqub (عَلَيْهِمَاٱلسَّلَامُ),

وَوَصَّىٰ بِهَآ إِبْرَٰهِـۧمُ بَنِيهِ وَيَعْقُوبُ يَٰبَنِيَّ إِنَّ ٱللَّهَ
ٱصْطَفَىٰ لَكُمُ ٱلدِّينَ فَلَا تَمُوتُنَّ إِلَّا وَأَنتُم مُّسْلِمُونَ
۝ أَمْ كُنتُمْ شُهَدَآءَ إِذْ حَضَرَ يَعْقُوبَ ٱلْمَوْتُ إِذْ قَالَ
لِبَنِيهِ مَا تَعْبُدُونَ مِنۢ بَعْدِى قَالُوا۟ نَعْبُدُ إِلَٰهَكَ
وَإِلَٰهَ ءَابَآئِكَ إِبْرَٰهِـۧمَ وَإِسْمَٰعِيلَ وَإِسْحَٰقَ إِلَٰهًا وَٰحِدًا
وَنَحْنُ لَهُۥ مُسْلِمُونَ ۝

"And this (submission to Allāh, Islām) was enjoined by 'Ibrāhīm (Abraham) upon his sons and by Ya'qūb (Jacob), (saying), 'O my sons! Allāh has chosen for you the (true) religion, then die not except in the Faith of Islām (as Muslims – Islāmic Monotheism).' Or were you witnesses when death approached Ya'qūb (Jacob)? When he said unto his sons, 'What will you worship after me?' They said, 'We shall worship your *Ilah* (God – Allāh), the *Ilah* (God) of your fathers, 'Ibrāhīm (Abraham), Ismā'il (Ishmael), Ishāq (Isaac), One *Ilah* (God), and to Him, we submit (in Islām).'" [*Sūrah al-Baqarah* 2:132-133]

The Lord of all that exists praises His Prophet Ismā'il (عَلَيْهِالسَّلَامُ) because he would order his family to pray and pay the Zakāt. Allāh (سُبْحَانَهُوَتَعَالَى) says,

$$﴿ وَكَانَ يَأْمُرُ أَهْلَهُ بِٱلصَّلَوٰةِ وَٱلزَّكَوٰةِ ﴾$$

"And he used to enjoin on his family and his people As-Salāh (the prayers) and the Zakāt." [*Sūrah Maryam* 19:55]

Allāh (سُبْحَانَهُوَتَعَالَى) ordered His Prophet Muḥammad (صَلَّىٱللَّهُعَلَيْهِوَسَلَّمَ) to preserve the performance of the obligatory prayers and that he order his family with the same as well as urge them to perform it just as Allāh (سُبْحَانَهُوَتَعَالَى) said,

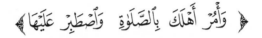

"And enjoin *As-Ṣalāh* (the prayer) on your family, and be patient in offering them [i.e. the *Ṣalāh* (prayers)]." [*Sūrah Taha* 20:132]

What is also included in the Prophets' guidance and sincere advice is that the father keeps his children away from anything that corrupts their morals and religion. For example, listening to music, harmful TV channels, and impermissible instruments; and in that way, he should be cautious of taking his children to impermissible places of amusement.

THE RIGHTEOUS COMPANION

Indeed, the children's covenant in the area of companionship and friendship is from the greatest supportive pillars in which cultivation is imperative.

Thus, the companion will drag (you), and it inevitably will have an impact in his companionship.

The Prophet (صَلَّ اللَّهُ عَلَيْهِ وَسَلَّمَ) gave us a parable expounding on the effects of the companion on his comrade pertaining to good and evil. He (صَلَّ اللَّهُ عَلَيْهِ وَسَلَّمَ) said,

مَثَلُ الْجَلِيسِ الصَّالِحِ وَالسَّوْءِ كَحَامِلِ الْمِسْكِ وَنَافِخِ الْكِيرِ، فَحَامِلُ الْمِسْكِ إِمَّا أَنْ يُحْذِيَكَ، وَإِمَّا أَنْ تَبْتَاعَ مِنْهُ، وَإِمَّا أَنْ تَجِدَ مِنْهُ رِيحًا طَيِّبَةً، وَنَافِخُ الْكِيرِ إِمَّا أَنْ يُحْرِقَ ثِيَابَكَ، وَإِمَّا أَنْ تَجِدَ رِيحًا خَبِيثَةً

"The example of a good pious companion and an evil one is that of a person carrying musk and another a blacksmith. The one who is carrying musk will either give you some

perfume as a present, or you will buy some from him, or you will get a good smell from him, but the blacksmith will either burn your clothes, or you will get a bad smell from him."[18]

The Prophet (ﷺ) said,

الْمَرْءُ عَلَى دِينِ خَلِيلِهِ فَلْيَنْظُرْ أَحَدُكُمْ مَنْ يُخَالِلُ

"A man is upon the religion of his friend; so each one should look to whom he takes as his friend." [19]

Hence, it is a must for the parents to watch whom their children take as a friend and accompany in school, etc. and visit at those places.

A new type of companion and friend has come into existence in this era which has not existed

---

[18] Collected by al-Bukhārī in his Ṣaḥīḥ (#5534), and Muslim in his Ṣaḥīḥ (#2628).
[19] Collected by Abū Dāwud in his book as-Sunan (#4833); also look in Shaykh al-Albānī's book as-Silsilah as-Ṣaḥīḥah (927).

in previous times. Yet, it is inconsiderable pertaining to its influence on the person from before. It is satellite TV, websites and social media via smartphones which children can carry in their hands wherever they are, whether in their homes or while outside.

These devices, if they are not under the supervision and observation of parents, can be immensely dangerous to their minds, religion, morals and etiquettes. How many have been ruined and deviated among the young men and women because of it?

The matter will lead them into enormous evil and grave calamities which none but Allāh (سُبْحَانَهُوَتَعَالَى) knows the true extent.

AN EXCELLENT EXAMPLE

Among the great supportive pillars (in cultivating children) is that the father is an example for his children. So when he commands them to do good, he should seek to embark upon it, and when he forbids them from evil, he should be the furthest from it.

Thus, his speech shouldn't say one thing, and his actions are say another; He is rearing the children upon contradiction, disharmony and enormous chaos from which the children are led into abandoning and disregarding guidance and cultivation from their father.

Let us recall Allāh's (سُبْحَانَهُوَتَعَالَى) statement to the children of Israel,

﴿ ۞ أَتَأْمُرُونَ ٱلنَّاسَ بِٱلْبِرِّ وَتَنسَوْنَ أَنفُسَكُمْ وَأَنتُمْ تَتْلُونَ ٱلْكِتَبَ أَفَلَا تَعْقِلُونَ ۝ ﴾

"Enjoin you *Al-Birr* (piety and righteousness and each and every act of obedience to Allāh) on the people, and you forget (to practice it) yourselves, while you recite the Scripture [the Taurat (Torah)]! Have you then no sense?" [*Sūrah al-Baqarah* 2:44]

Also, look at the Prophet of Allāh, Shuʿayb's statement (عَلَيْهِٱلسَّلَامُ) to his people,

﴿ وَمَآ أُرِيدُ أَنْ أُخَالِفَكُمْ إِلَىٰ مَا أَنْهَىٰكُمْ عَنْهُ ﴾

"I wish not, in contradiction to you, to do that which I forbid you." [*Sūrah Hud* 11:88]

Allāh (سُبْحَانَهُۥوَتَعَالَىٰ) also says,

﴿ يَٰٓأَيُّهَا ٱلَّذِينَ ءَامَنُوا۟ لِمَ تَقُولُونَ مَا لَا تَفْعَلُونَ ۝ كَبُرَ مَقْتًا عِندَ ٱللَّهِ أَن تَقُولُوا۟ مَا لَا تَفْعَلُونَ ۝ ﴾

"O you who believe! Why do you say that which you do not do? Most hateful it is with

Allāh that you say that which you do not do."
[*Sūrah Saff* 61:2-3]

The scholars have mentioned that following examples where actions speak for themselves is more profound than following mere speech (i.e., without action).

This is just a short summary of the supportive pillars which will aid in the cultivating, educating and good upbringing of children. The Muslim should understand that he must show great concern and attention to these supportive pillars and apply them as well.

Thus, he will become the first to reap the fruits of this cultivation both during his lifetime and after his death. As for in his lifetime, his child becomes righteous and dutiful; one who preserves the rights of his parents and avoids unruliness to them. This is because Islām, which he was cultivated upon, orders and urges him to do that.

As for after his death, his child will go to great lengths to supplicate for his father. The Prophet (عَلَيْهِ الصَّلَاةُ وَٱلسَّلَامُ) said,

إِذَا مَاتَ ابْنُ آدَمَ انْقَطَعَ عَنْهُ عَمَلُهُ إِلاَّ مِنْ ثَلاَثٍ: صَدَقَةٍ جَارِيَةٍ، وَ عِلْمٍ يُنْتَفَعُ بِهِ، وَ وَلَدٍ صَالِحٍ يَدْعُو لَهُ

"When a man dies, his deeds come to an end, but three, recurring charity, or knowledge (by which people) benefit, or a pious son, who prays for him (for the deceased)."[20]

It is our duty to call this matter to our attention as the matter of cultivating children is an immense and grave one. It is incumbent upon every father to give extra consideration to it.

Indeed, the most common corruption of the children is caused by the parents' neglect and abandonment of them.

Al-Allamah ibn al-Qayyim (رَحِمَهُ ٱللَّهُ) said,

"Whoever neglects to educate his child as to what benefits and has had his child in vain, then he has done the utmost evil act. Corruption of most children comes from the parents neglecting them and abandoning

---

[20] Collected by Muslim in his Ṣaḥīḥ (#1631).

teaching them the obligatory and sunan matters of the religion."

There is an important matter which is mandatory for the father to call to mind and that is that even with taking great care of these means and supportive pillars in cultivating his children, it is incumbent upon him to entrust his affair to Allāh (جَلَّجَلَالُه), having true reliance in Him. He should not attach his heart to the means alone. Rather he must entrust his affair to Allāh and have true reliance alone in the betterment and preservation of his children with what Allāh preserves in His righteous servants.

Shaykh ibn Uthaymīn (رَحِمَهُٱللَّه) said,

"I don't believe that anyone who has Taqwā of Allāh regarding his children and follows the path of Islāmic legislation in guiding them except that Allāh (سُبْحَانَهُوَتَعَالَى) guides his children." [21]

I ask Allāh to aid us all in cultivating and guiding our children in the correct manner, and may He

---

[21] Fatawa Nūr ala ad-Darb (2/24).

rectify them and protect them from evident and hidden trials, and may He make them leaders of guidance, not those who are misled and leading others astray—Indeed Allāh is all-Hearing and responds to supplications.

May Allāh raise the rank our Prophet Muḥammad and grant him, his family, and his Companions peace.

Made in the USA
Columbia, SC
02 August 2021

42477494R00031